Pursue, Overtake, and Reclaim
A Divine Strategy for Victory

Bishop Andrew Merritt

Pursue, Overtake, and Reclaim: A Divine Strategy for Victory
©1992, 2018 Andrew Merritt

Unless otherwise indicated, all Scripture quotations are taken from the King James Version of the Holy Bible.

Bishop Andrew Merritt Ministries
www.bishopmerrittministries.org

ISBN 13: 978-0-9637640-6-5

All rights reserved.

No part of this book may be reproduced in any manner whatsoever, without written permission from Bishop Andrew Merritt Ministries.

Printed in the United States of America.

DEDICATION

To Viveca,
my darling wife,
partner, and friend.

With special thanks to
Karen V. Brown and Charlotte H. O'Connor

TABLE OF CONTENTS

Foreword	7
A Militant Church	9
Pursue the Enemy	15
Overtake the Enemy	19
Reclaim All	21
Paul's Example	28
Use Your Weapons	35
David's Example	37
What Belongs to You That the Devil Has Taken?	44
Total Victory	46
The Invitation	47

FOREWORD

It's time...time for the Church of the Living God to **pursue, overtake, and reclaim** everything the enemy has stolen from us!

For too long we have allowed the devil to wreak havoc in our lives. Jesus is coming back for a mature church, and we cannot afford to sit by idly any longer and allow Satan to exercise authority in our lives. **We must declare war on our enemy!**

We must become a more militant church! We must begin to recognize not only who we are, but Whose we are and live in that revelation. Once we seize hold to this revelation, we will begin to walk and rest in God's ordination for us—**TOTAL VICTORY!**

We must remember that the devil is ALWAYS defeated! No matter what your circumstance is, his position and destiny will never change.

PURSUE, OVERTAKE, AND RECLAIM reveals truths that are based on the infallible, unchangeable Word of God. This book will reveal to you the God-given authority invested in every believer.

So often we box God in. Many of us were taught that it's OK to lose a battle, as long as you win the war. That's wrong! The Holy Spirit was sent so you can stand victoriously amid your most severe trial. God has given His church a divine strategy for victory—walk in it!

I pray that after reading **PURSUE, OVERTAKE, AND RECLAIM** you will be stirred to go into the enemy's camp and take back what rightfully belongs to you.

God Bless You.

Bishop Andrew Merritt

A MILITANT CHURCH

The problem with the people of God is they are not looking for their enemy. Instead, their enemy is looking for them. The church of the Lord Jesus Christ is called to be militant, not defensive. God's word says in Proverbs 6:31, "But if he be found, he shall restore sevenfold; he shall give all the substance of his house." **If he be found,** ...we're supposed to be looking for satan, not satan looking for us.

You can't be a Sunday morning saint, passive and indecisive, sitting on the sidelines, and expect to walk in victory. The devil will come against you and overtake you; he will strip you and literally try to destroy you. But that is not God's plan for you.

Walking in victory is God's plan for you, and that is why He gave you His armor. **The armor of God—** the helmet of salvation, breastplate of righteousness, feet shod with the preparation of the Gospel of peace, loins girded about with truth, shield of faith, the sword of the Spirit (which is the Word of God) – protects us in the battle against the enemy. Notice how God never made provisions for your back. **We are not a retreating church!**

A minister once said, "If you can't do anything, crawl." No...God never said crawl. He said, "Fight!" See trying to appeal to your emotions is not good enough. What you need is truth! It's the truth that sets you free. If you know who you are, then you know God is in you, and you are in God. We don't crawl anywhere...we run through troops and leap over walls. In **your** advancement (not the devil's) you go toward him. While he's literally shooting fiery darts at you, he's wondering how you can keep coming at him!

You have an invisible shield. Satan doesn't understand that because he's not a child of faith. But you are, and no matter what he shoots at you, you can lift your shield of faith and quench the fiery darts of the wicked. You keep on coming because you're after something.

1 Peter 5:8 says, "...the devil, as a roaring lion, walketh about, seeking whom he may devour." Satan walks around **as** a roaring lion, but he's not a roaring lion. He's an imposter! Jesus, the **Lion** of the tribe of Judah, has pulled his teeth. The only thing the devil can do to you is gum you.

Just as God seeks men to worship Him in spirit and truth, Satan seeks those whom he can devour. But the only person, the devil, can devour is a person who doesn't really know who he is. I know who I am in God.

Now, don't get mad at me because I know who I am in God. Don't get mad at me because I know the Lord has made me promises in His word. He said, "Son, I'm with you always, even until the end of the world [or the end of the age] (Matthew 28:20); Greater is He that is in you than he that is in the world (1 John 4:4); If God be for us, who [in the world] can be against us" (Romans 8:31). God has promised to be my light and salvation—who shall I fear? (Psalm 27:1). 2 Timothy says For God hath not given us the spirit of fear, but of power, and love, and of a sound mind (a normal mind in the Spirit of God)."

I have no fear because fear brings torment. Instead of torment, I have peace, joy, strength, grace, the ability of God, and the Spirit of God.

Because God is my Father, He didn't just put me out he unclothed. Everything He is, He put in me! If you're going to go on in the things of God, one thing must be established. We know the devil is a thief, that he's walking around seeking people to devour. But you really need to understand that satan is a **bad** guy. Say this out loud—**the devil is a bad guy!**

Some preacher is going to come along and tell you God is bad. God's not bad. God is totally good! Some preacher may try to tell you that God is the source of all your problems. That's a lie! God doesn't run your children down with a truck, and God doesn't put cancer on you. God doesn't put cancer on you because He doesn't even have any cancer. The only way God can put cancer on you is if He were to steal it. God just doesn't have any sickness or disease.

Now what the minister said to you, he said for a reason. He said it to cover himself. If I drop dead because of sickness and disease, that has nothing to do with what God says. God has gone on record (even before I came into this earth) saying, "...He [God] shall bless thy bread, and thy water; and I will take sickness away from the midst of thee," (Exodus 23:25).

Some people think that the Church has a 'worse' covenant that Israel had. That's simply not true. Israel was a slave, **but we are sons**. Israel was just a servant. When God brought the Israelites out of Egypt, **He brought them out with not so much as a sick, feeble one among them.** How can you be sick when you have the glory of God on you all day and all night?

Now for all of those who have a poverty mindset, God gave me a revelation the other day that blew me away. (I wonder why some folks can't teach by revelation.) I was sitting studying, and just meditating on the Word of God when the Lord gave me another insight. God said to me, "Son when I brought Israel out, I brought them out to be kings and queens. But their slave mentality locked them into being slaves."

That slave mentality is like a similar illustration once given by Clinton White, a New York minister. A polar bear in Europe was housed in a cage. The cage was 11 feet long and 11 feet wide, and the bear was accustomed to going 11 feet up and 11 feet back. One day the bear was purchased and shipped to another country. He was released in a great environment, having much space and no bars. You know what happened? That polar bear only went 11 feet up and 11 feet back.

That type of mentality is found in the church. People speak in tongues and still only walk 11 feet up and 11 feet back. They're chained to their past: to bad doctrine, traditions, commandments, and teachings of men. Yet God says, "...and forgetting those things which are behind," (Philippians 3:13). In other words, God is the God of the universe, and there's a whole world out there to explore! Some of you need to take a vacation and break out of that 11 feet up and 11 feet back rut.

The Lord said to me, through the Spirit of God, "Most ministers who talk about Israel coming out [of Egypt] don't even have it half right." When the Israelites left Egypt, they stripped Egypt. Egypt didn't just give them gold; they also left wearing fine clothes and jewels. And they walked in those clothes for 40 years! God did His best to try and get them to understand the Scripture, "I brought you out to be the head and not the tail, and thou shall be above only, and thou shall not be beneath...to lend and not borrow," (Deuteronomy 28:23; 15:6). They had the presence of God by day in a pillar of a cloud and by night in a pillar of fire, and when they needed water, God provided it. When they were hungry, He gave them fresh manna. Yet they stayed locked into their past.

Right now, Jesus has provision ready for your health, your children, your church, your city, your nation, and the world. But you must arise and understand that God has settled and signed for you to be the overcomer—not to succumb, but to overcome!

PURSUE THE ENEMY

To pursues means to follow in order to overtake or capture, to chase, to strive for, and to seek after. The devil has something that belongs to you. You're not to allow him to take it—you're to go after what he has taken!

Now Jesus said, "...I am come that they might have life and that they might have it more abundantly," (John 10:10). He also said, "The thief cometh not, but to steal, and to kill, and to destroy." The devil's desire is to destroy you. He will steal from you, and he will kill you. But if the thief be found, "...he shall restore sevenfold..." (Proverbs 6:31). Seven is the number of completion—God's perfect number. He shall restore sevenfold and "...he shall give all the substance of his house."

He said, "...but if he be found..." This indicates to me if I apply the rule of what I call 'necessary emphasis," that I must seek him. Instead of the devil looking for me, I must go looking for him. The church has problems because we allow satan to see us out; we ought to seek him out and put your foot on his head!

The devil may be cunning but let me share something with you—**he's also stupid!** Now don't worry about saying that. You don't have to be quiet. You don't have to be afraid. **HE'S STUPID!** Do you want to know why? If you read the Bible, you'll find out. I've read the end of the Book, and I found out we win!

But the devil is still fighting. Anybody that has already been beaten has had his authority taken away, and is still fighting, is stupid! The Scripture said, "...had they known it, they would not have crucified the Lord of glory," (1 Corinthians 2:8).

The devil's main power was death. Jesus, by His death, conquered death. Jesus said, "I...have the keys of hell and of death," (Revelation 1:18). "All power in heaven and earth is given unto me," said God.

However, the devil is only stupid to the who know him—not to the man **who** has a veil over his eyes. The Bible says, "...the whole world lieth in wickedness," (1 John 5:19). All those whom the devil has deceived by a lie, he has in the palm of his hand—he can manipulate them. But when you know who he is, **Satan cannot touch you!**

We're talking about the spirit world. Remember when the sons of Sceva tried to cast out that demon and the demon rose up and said, "...Jesus, I know, and Paul I know; but who are ye?" (Acts 19:15). In other words, the demon was saying,

"Here is somebody who isn't even filled with the Holy Spirit. We only obey those who are filled with the Holy Spirit and **use** authority. We don't pay any attention to those who have the Holy Spirit and **don't use** their authority—those are the ones we devour!"

Satan is looking for the man who carries the Word of God under his arm and **never** reads it. People who come to church, are filled with the Spirit of God, never read the Word, and never come back, will just be devoured by the devil. He will rob them, taking their money, children, husbands, wives, jobs; and they really won't know what's happening to them. Those are the ones Satan seeks out. He's not looking for those who walk around saying, "Greater is He that is in me, than he that is in the world;" or those who stand up with the Spirit of boldness and say, "Our God is able;" or those who know that Jesus is the Prince of the kings of the Earth, the King of kings, and the Lord of lords. Satan is not looking for those who know the truth, that through His blood **Jesus destroyed sin** and settled the sin question once and for all!

Through the power of the Spirit of God, Jesus said, "...He that believeth on me, the works that I do shall he do also, and **greater** works than these shall he do; because I go unto my Father...that the Father may be glorified," (John 14:12-13).

Because you're going to do greater works, the devil is terrified of you! **So, you need to be looking for him.** You need to pursue him, and if he be found, you should **demand he restore** sevenfold. Everything he has, you can get—**sevenfold blessings!**

OVERTAKE THE ENEMY

The church needs to learn how to overtake. It means to catch up with and go beyond, to surely take hold of, to capture. When the devil comes after your children, you'd better catch up with him, and catch up quick! And not only catch up with him but **overtake him!** The first time your children start coughing, you'd better be on his case.

We need to understand what the devil is trying to do. It's just like sickness and disease—the first time you get a symptom, **don't claim it!** Don't sign for that package—curse it and tell him to take it back. You'd better **overtake it**. You need to go after him—to come upon, to go beyond.

What would you do if you suddenly came home and caught me in your home, stealing? Would you rationalize that I'm a pastor and a nice man? No, you'd come to grips with reality and say, "What are you doing in my house? You must be a thief! What are you looking for?" I might tell you that you left the key in the door, but you wouldn't buy that either. And this is what we have to do with the devil. If the devil. If the devil has taken anything from you, you need to pursue him, overtake him, and reclaim that which he has taken. Don't buy his lies!

RECLAIM ALL

The word reclaim means to rescue; to bring back someone from error; to make what once was wasteland capable of being cultivated or lived on, to be made whole. We're to take back what satan has taken from us. We're to **reclaim** all our possessions.

There are many of us from whom the devil has stolen. He's taken our health, our finances, and our children (through drugs, alcohol, and abuse). He's even moved in the area of our jobs.

Many of you are terrified by fear. Satan has come out against you, and you don't understand that the more ground you yield, the more he takes. You need to quit being on the defensive and **go on the offensive.**

The Bible says in Matthew 18:18, "...whatsoever ye shall bind on earth shall be bound in heaven: and whatsoever ye loose on earth shall be loosed in heaven." In Greek, it says, "...whatsoever you bind on earth is already bound, whatsoever you loose in the earth is already loosed." And in Matthew 12:29 Jesus also said, "...except he first bind the strong man...and then he will spoil his house..."

Isn't it nice and wonderful to come to church sick and let somebody else bind the devil for you and you get healed? Now that will work for a while because God knows you're a little child. But once you get to be 50 years old, He expects you to act like you're 50.

Let's read what Luke 11:9-13 says:

And I say unto you, Ask, and it shall be given you; seek, and ye shall find; knock, and it shall be opened unto you. **10** For every one that asketh [no one is excluded—all are included] receiveth; and he that seeketh findeth, and to him that knocketh it shall be opened. **11** If a son shall ask bread of any of you that is a father, will he give him a stone? or if he asks a fish, will he for a fish give him a serpent [something that would hurt him]? **12** Or if he shall ask an egg, will he offer him a scorpion? **13** If ye then, being **evil** [underline the word **'evil'**; it means unrighteous. It's not in reference to believers, but it's in reference to the human family.], know how to give **good** gifts [note the word 'good'] unto your children: how much **more** [not just the same, but more, because God doesn't deal with us according to the relationship we have with our natural fathers—He supersedes any father that's in this earth!] shall your heavenly Father give the Holy Spirit to them that ask him?

Now it could be the baptism of the Holy Spirit that you're asking for, speaking with other tongues as the Spirit of God gives utterance, or it could be a manifestation of the Spirit of God. The gifts of the Spirit are manifestations of the Spirit.

When the Spirit of God goes into operation, He desires to go into operation for you. When people say, "I have the **gift** of the **manifestation** of the **spirituality** of God," they are zoning in on only one manifestation of spiritual gifts. God had so much more to offer: "...how much more shall God give the Holy Spirit to them that ask?" In other words, **whatever you need the Holy Spirit will provide.**

While you're reading this book, right now, **God will provide for you.** If you need healing, you don't have to wait until an altar call is made at church. You reach out—**right now**—and, activate by faith the gifts of miracles and healings. **God can meet your needs right now!** Some of you go to church burdened down, needing to hear from God. You can hear from God NOW because your faith can activate God's word.

These gifts of God **should** be operating in your life: the word of wisdom, the word of knowledge, and **especially** discernment of spirits.

We wouldn't make half the mistakes we make if we'd operate the gift of **discernment of spirits**. God gave us that gift to be manifested. **We need that gift.**

Thank God for tongues and interpretations of tongues, but we must go way beyond that. "If ye then, being evil, know how to give good gifts unto your children, how much more shall your heavenly Father give the Holy Spirit to them that ask?"

We are after the devil! If you need a physical manifestation of the power of God—healing or deliverance—and you need to be set free by the power of God, **hear the Word of the Lord.**

Jesus went to church just like we do. The first time Jesus went to church after His baptism, He really upset the church. Until that time, he was just a nice young man who went to the synagogue, studied the Scriptures, and did the reading. But after His baptism by John and His wilderness experience, **Jesus went back to the church a changed man.** The Scriptures says in Luke 4:17, "And there was delivered unto him the book of the prophet Esaias. And when he had opened the book, he found the place where it was written..." This time He didn't read the same way. **This time He had authority and power!** The devil is afraid of people who operate with authority; he's not afraid of those who don't know the Word of God.

So, Jesus stood up to read. "...He found the place where it was written, 'The Spirit of the Lord is upon Me...'" With that announcement, all the people said, "Huh!" They hadn't heard about the Spirit of the Lord being on anyone since Malachi—approximately 430 years before! Oh, they knew about John, but they really weren't sure that John was a prophet. When Jesus said the Spirit of the Lord was upon Him, boldly regarding, "...He has anointed Me...," and stepped out of the crowd, He was stepping out on the Word of God and demonstrating His belief in it. He didn't leave the people unsure of what the Scripture meant; He showed them what it meant.

While you're in the crowd, nothing is going to happen. When you're passive and indecisive, nothing is going to happen. If you're a 'Sunday Saint,' carrying a Bible on a buddy-buddy plan with somebody, nothing is going to happen. But when you step out of the crowd, becoming decisive and stepping on the Word of God, the **Anointing** will come—just like it did with Jesus!

Jesus said, "The Spirit of the Lord is upon Me because He has anointed me to preach the Gospel to the poor…" The Gospel is Good News to the poor and I have Good News for you—you don't have to be poor! Jesus was poor that you might become rich (2 Corinthians 8:9).

Luke 4:20 reads, "…and the eyes of all them that were in the synagogue were fastened on him." You know, the people must have wondered, murmuring among themselves and saying something like, "We know who you are. You were born of fornication. We know Mary, and we know Joseph. You are an imposter."

They took Jesus to the brow of the hill to kill Him. Luke 4:30 reads, "But he passing through the midst of them went his way." Let me share something with you: whenever God tells you to do something, God is in it, and before you make the first step, **He's already made a way of deliverance for you.** PRAISE GOD!

One Sabbath, Jesus went into the synagogue and found a woman who had been bound by a spirit that was not of God (Luke 13). Now the Bible says that Jesus was **anointed** with the Holy Ghost and with power and that he went about doing good and healing all that were oppressed of the devil. The Bible also says that **God was with Him**. So here's a woman—locked in a bent-over-position—bound by the devil for 18 years!

Now before Jesus healed her, He spoke to the religious leaders. Jesus wanted to know what **was going on with them.** Because for 18 years they had not allowed this woman to come into the synagogue and remain bound by the devil. They didn't **pursue** her healing; they didn't **overtake** the devil, and they didn't **reclaim** the restoration of her body. Yet the Bible says in Daniel 11:32, "...the people that do know their God shall be strong and do exploits." **Jesus took control, exercised His authority, and cast that spirit of infirmity out of that woman!** We can only be strong and do exploits for God if we've been with Him.

PAUL'S EXAMPLE

In Acts, chapter 16, Paul was in Philippi. He preached the Gospel and people were saved. Paul was put in jail for this. Verse 25 states, "And at midnight Paul and Silas prayed, and sang praises unto God: and the prisoners heard them." Now most people found in this type of situation would cry, and not even be able to think about praising God. Yet the Bible says in Philippians 4:4, "Rejoice in the Lord always[s]..." When you deny the power of God, when you have pity parties, you focus the attention on yourself. Instead of asking, "Why me Lord? Say, 'Thank you God for this opportunity—I'm in a good place for you to manifest your power and glory!"

Do you know what the word grace means? Grace does mean God's unmerited favor, but there is another definition. Grace is also **God's willingness to use His power and ability on your behalf.** And God never runs out of grace. James 4:6 says, "But He giveth more grace."

God wants us to focus in on him, just like Paul and Silas did—they sang praises unto God. Imagine what they might have sung—"The joy of the Lord is my strength...," and then worshipped and prayed, singing in the Spirit. Imagine them making harmony unto the Lord, the vibrations of their voices blending with such power, such force, that the foundation began to tremble.

That's how to get delivered—singing the praises of God. Don't talk about fear, doubt, and unbelief. Just sing the praises of God! Their feet were in stocks, and they were in pain, but that didn't stop them from praising God. **Let every fiber of your being praise Him, for He's worthy of EVERY praise!**

We see in Acts 16: 25-30 that Paul and Silas were praising God. Most people were asleep at midnight, but not heaven—THERE WAS ACTION IN HEAVEN!

And at midnight Paul and Silas prayed, and sang praises unto God: and the prisoners heard them.

> ^{26}And suddenly there was a great earthquake, so that the foundations of the prison were shaken: and immediately all the doors were opened, and every one's bands were loosed [That's heaven in action!].^{27} And the keeper of the prison awaking out of his sleep, and seeing the prison doors open, he drew out his sword, and would have killed himself, supposing that the prisoners had been fled. ^{28} But Paul cried with a loud voice, saying, Do thyself

no harm: for we are all here. ²⁹ Then he called for a light, and sprang in, and came trembling, and fell down before Paul and Silas, ³⁰ And brought them out, and said, Sirs, what must I do to be saved?"

You see, when you worship God, standing the test and staying there, **people are affected by your witness**. They don't see you retreat; they don't see you fall, and they don't see you fold under the pressure that the devil applies—**they see you stand!**

Let me tell you something: Any pressure that the devil applies is not against you—it's against Who's in you! You must remember that you can fall, but God can **NEVER** be defeated. The devil doesn't care about you, and he doesn't care about me. He despises God Who is in you. It's a spiritual thing. It has nothing to do with race, intellect, or looks. Satan is trying to separate you from your God. He's trying to get the Word out of you, to get you off the Word of God.

The Bible teaches that satan, who is the thief, only comes to steal, kill, and destroy (John 10:10). When the Word of God is sown, the devil comes **immediately** to challenge the Word.

In Acts 16:30-31, the keeper of the prison said, "...what must I do to be saved? And they said, 'Believe on the Lord Jesus Christ, and thou shalt be saved **and thy house.**'"

The devil still has something that God promised to you!

God didn't just promise to save you—**He also promised to save your household**. The only person who has those of your household is the devil. You ought to rise up and talk to that old rascal. Call him a thief. Tell him like it is. Get down to the naked bone, the nitty-gritty. Tell him that Jesus whipped him, pulled his teeth, and took the power and authority from him. Tell him, "In the name of Jesus, **I bind you in that person's life.**" Command him to release that person. Until that happens, until you **pursue, overtake, and reclaim** your folks are going to die and go to hell.

God said, in Ezekiel 22:30, "And I sought for a man among them, that should make up the hedge and stand in the gap before me for the land, that I should not destroy it, but I found none."

An **intercessor** is a person who takes the place of, or stands in the gap on behalf of, another. I'm not talking about praying the prayer of petition. I'm talking about intercession. You can stand in the presence of God for a person, but you can also turn and face the devil and tell him—**No!** You can't have this person!" Stand in the gap for all of our young people. Tell the devil he can't have them. Even if they're on crack, drugs, alcohol, or running with guns—tell satan he still can't have them! Tell the devil, **"You can't have them. I come against you; not in my strength, but in the NAME that's above every name—THE NAME OF JESUS!"**

Often, we talk too much, and we talk about the wrong things. We're not to talk about problems, fear, and calamities; we're to speak blessings and favor. We're not to promote what the devil is doing. We're not to help satan devour. We're to stand in the gap and make up the hedge. Romans 15:1 says, "We then that are strong ought to bear the infirmities of the weak, and not to please ourselves. We're not to see someone down and keep our feet on him.

That's the problem with the Church today. We don't have enough spiritual people. Galatians 6:1 says, "...if man [brother] be overtaken in a fault, ye which are spiritual, restore such a one in the spirit of meekness; considering thyself, lest thou also be tempted."

In Acts 16:31 we read, "...Believe on the Lord Jesus Christ, and thou shalt be saved, and thy house."

Every time your saved relatives close their eyes and leave this earth, it saddens the heart of God. You may say, "Well, they weren't saved, and they didn't want to be saved," but how do you know that? God didn't tell you to be so intellectual that you try to figure out whether a person wants to be saved or not. As far as you're concerned, until they take their last breath, they want to be saved!

Years ago, when I first came to the Lord, an evangelist came to minister in our little church. A lady who was under the influence of alcohol came into the meeting. The minister began to speak to her saying, "You are reprobate, and God's not interested in you." Now I was just young in the Lord at that time, but I knew that wasn't right! The minister was supposed to be speaking through the Spirit of God, but I knew that wasn't of God. Only God knows if a man is a reprobate. My purpose is to try to get folks saved, not to run them out of church.

Babies are born every day. Hospitals are filled with them. As they grow and develop, they start to walk—they start to stumble around. That's just how it is in the church. Babies are being born into the body of Christ every day, being filled with the Holy Spirit. And just like natural babies, people in the church are at various stages of development, walking around and stumbling, but just because you're stumbling doesn't mean God has rejected you. God still loves you. The fact is, He loves you so much, He's already made a provision for you.

Jesus' death was God's provision for us. Jesus died for our sins and said that if we fail on this side of the cross, we can be forgiven. 1 John 1:9 says, "If we confess our sins, He is faithful and just to forgive us our sins, and cleanse us from all unrighteousness." God's not going to throw you away. You can throw God away, but God's not going to throw you away.

USE YOUR WEAPONS

You're going to have to do something about the devil. And it's going to have to be **pursuing, overtaking,** and **reclaiming** all that he's taken from you. We're in a war, and it's no time to be ignoring the truth of God's Word. **The Word of God is our weapon,** and we're to use it to fight against and defeat the enemy.

When I was in the military, I spent eight weeks learning how to fire an M-1 rifle. They assigned it to us, taught us how to clean it, and how to fire it. After that, because they wanted us to understand how important this weapon was to us, they told us, "If the gun jams on you in combat because of your negligence, it will cost you your life!" That was serious stuff, and so we learned how to keep it clean and use it. Since all truth is parallel, if we don't learn how to use the Sword of the Spirit, which is the Word of God, we'll perish just like the soldier who doesn't learn how to use his weapon. **We will never be able to pursue, overtake, and reclaim if we don't know how to use God's Word as a weapon.**

Being a child of God does not save us from adversity. **Adversity comes because you are a child of God.** God knows you're going through problems and He sits patiently in expectation, ready to move on your behalf. 1 Corinthians 10:13 says, "There hath no temptation taken you, but such as is common to man: but God is faithful, who will not suffer you to be tempted above that ye are able; but will with the temptation also make a way to escape, that ye may be able to bear it." When the temptation comes, even before it comes, right when satan thinks of it, **God has already made a way of escape for you!** God has gone way ahead of satan and knowing the ending from the beginning, knows the very moment the temptation enters satan's mind.

The devil doesn't have an original thought in his mind. Everything the devil has he's perverted. **The devil misrepresents everything!** He takes God's original thoughts and changes them into perversions. For faith, he tries to bring fear. For life, he tries to bring death. Satan left the truth and perverted it until it became error. When speaking about satan, Jesus said in John 8:44, "...and abode not in the truth..." Satan went to the opposite extreme. While God says life, health, prosperity, and blessings, satan tries to change it into death, sickness, poverty, and calamities. Death is the absence of the life of God. **Don't listen to satan's lies!**

DAVID'S EXAMPLE

Let's look at the life of David. He was a man after God's own heart, and there are some things in his life that we need to consider.

God sent the prophet Samuel to the house of Jesse to anoint the next king of Israel. God rejected Saul because of his sin, and God sought another king. Now God had already chosen David, but no one, not even Samuel knew it. God rejected each of those brothers until David was brought before Samuel. "This is he; this is my choice," God said. The little shepherd boy was anointed with oil to become king of Israel.

Notice how God operates. While Saul was still king, God anointed David to become king. Israel has two kings—rejected king who still sat on the throne, and another one who had just been anointed to replace him. And you know what that shepherd boy did after he was anointed king of Israel? He went right back to tending the sheep. David was anointed with oil, but it wasn't time yet for him to ascend to the throne. If only we would learn, like David, that God promotes people and we can't be promoted in God before our time: "...promotion comes neither from the east nor from, the west, nor from the south. But God is the judge..." (Psalms 75:6-7).

David never did anything to take the throne away from Saul. What David did was to display the Spirit of God that rested upon him. When David was anointed with oil, he was anointed with the Spirit of God. He displayed it when he slew the lion, the bear, and Goliath. This demonstration of the power of God in David's life caused Saul to turn against him and persecute him.

You can see what is happening in the life of David. He was minding his own business, but because he was a man after God's own heart, God chose him to be king over Israel. What a position this placed David in! Anointed with the Spirit of God, he began to display the power of God in his life. And what suffering his new position brought into his life.

We see in 1 Samuel, chapter 30, where David and his men, upon returning from battle, found that the Amalekites had destroyed the Israelite camp and carried away the women and children: " And David was greatly distressed; for the people spake of stoning him, because the soul of all the people was grieved every man for his sons and his daughter, but **David encouraged himself in the Lord his God.**" If you're going to learn how to pursue overtake, and reclaim, you're going to have to

learn how to encourage yourself in God (not people).

Their camp was destroyed, their women and children carried away, and the men were weeping. What a situation! But the Scriptures say, in Psalm 30:5, "...weeping may endure for a night, but joy cometh in the morning." And Psalm 126:6 says, "He that goeth forth and weepeth, bearing precious seed..." In other words, the sorrow is going to end after a while!

There's a time to weep, and there's a time to grieve. But some saints have been grieving for 40 years. Every time you see them, they're grieving. There's a time for the release of your emotions, and grieving has its place. But there comes a time when you must put off grieving, **encourage yourself**, and move on to the new day.

When Israel started talking about stoning David, **David encouraged himself**. How does a man (or woman, boy, or girl) encourage himself? **Through meditation**. Meditation means to roll the Scripture over repeatedly in your mind.

When I'm going through trials and tribulations, **I begin to meditate.** I get a Scripture and begin to roll it over in my mind. If the Holy Spirit doesn't give me anything from that, I go back to my experiences. Like the day I was at Dodge Main automobile plant, where I worked. It was around 1:00 in the afternoon, and I was sitting in an open area when I heard the naked voice of God saying, "ANDREW, I'M CALLING YOU TO PREACH MY WORD." That's enough to keep anybody going!

The key to encouraging yourself is in being able to relate your experiences with God. When you look back and see where God has brought you from, that's enough to make you shout, dance, speak in tongues, and everything else. You'll find that **you can stand in the midst of the battle** when you learn to encourage yourself.

Remember David was going through. It looked as if everything was against him. Even his own people wanted to kill him. Yet he found something with which he could encourage himself. I imagine him sitting there thinking about the day Samuel came and poured that oil upon him. He probably thought about the lion he killed with his bare hands. No doubt he thought about the day of his greatest trial, when he took a little stone and in the name of Yahweh Jehovah, threw it out like a missile. David surely knew his God was in that missile, guiding it into the only uncovered spot on Goliath's head.

He probably considered the faith and courage of the young boy who supernaturally picked up his sword and cut off the giant's head.

David knew who he was and we must know who we are. When God has ordained something for you to do, **do not allow the devil to disrupt what God has originated!** Rise up through the Spirit of God and **pursue him, overtake him, and reclaim** that which he has stolen!

1 Samuel 30:8 says, "And David inquired at the Lord saying, 'Shall I pursue after this troop? Shall I overtake them?' And He answered him, '**Pursue**, for though shall surely **overtake** them and without fail **recover all**.'"

Let me share something with you—God doesn't want you to lose anything. Not one thing. That's why I'm bold; that's why I'm excited. I read the Word of God, and I found out He doesn't want you to lose anything. **Not one thing**!

1 Samuel 30:9-10 reads, "So David went, he and the six hundred men that were with him, and came to the brook Besor, where those that were left behind stayed. But David pursued, he and four hundred men: for two hundred abode behind, which we so faint that they could not go over the brook Besor."

We need to learn to pursue. Deuteronomy 32:30 says, "How should one chase a thousand, and two put ten thousand to flight, except their Rock had sold them..." And make sure the person praying with you knows how to believe God because the devil is not moved by talk.

I Samuel 30:11-18:

> **11** And they found an Egyptian in the field, and brought him to David, and gave him bread, and he did eat, and they made him drink water; **12** And they gave him a piece of a cake of figs, and two clusters of raisins: and when he had eaten, his spirit came again to him: for he had eaten no bread, nor drunk any water, three days and three nights. **13** And David said unto him, To whom belongest thou? and whence art thou? And he said, I am a young man of Egypt, servant to an Amalekite; and my master left me because three days agone I fell sick. **14** We made an invasion upon the south of the Cherethites, and upon the coast which belongeth to Judah, and upon the south of Caleb, and we burned Ziklag with fire. **15** And David said to him, Canst thou bring me down to this company? And he said, Swear unto me by God, that thou

wilt neither kill me, nor deliver me into the hands of my master, and I will bring thee down to this company. **16** And when he had brought him down, behold, they were spread abroad upon all the earth, eating and drinking, and dancing, because of all the great spoil that they had taken out of the land of the Philistines, and out of the land of Judah. **17** And David smote them from the twilight even unto the evening of the next day: and there escaped not a man of them, save four hundred young men, which rode upon camels, and fled."

And David recovered all that the Amalekites had carried away: and David rescued his two wives. David overcame them, and the next verse says, "And David recovered all..."

WHAT BELONGS TO YOU THAT THE DEVIL HAS TAKEN? WHAT ARE YOU GOING TO DO ABOUT IT?

1 Samuel 30:18-20: "And David recovered all that the Amalekites had carried away: and David rescued his two wives. And there was nothing lacking to them, neither small nor great, neither sons nor daughters, neither spoil nor anything that they had taken to them:" **David recovered all.** And David took all the flocks and the herds, which they drove before those other cattle, and said, 'This is David's spoil." David captured his enemies and took all that they had for himself. **When there's a battle, the victor gathers spoils.**

I remember when a preacher was talking to me about David and Goliath. He tried to make it sound as if you don't get anything when you engage in spiritual warfare. I shocked him when I said, "You never read the Bible!" Most people who carry Bibles don't read them. And just because you're a preacher, it doesn't mean you read it with understanding.

In the conquest of Goliath, when Goliath stood before Israel for forty days, challenging them, the whole Israeli army trembled. Everyone was afraid!

But then along came this freshly anointed boy named David. **David was bold.** He didn't just say, I'm going to go and fight the giant;" he also asked, "What shall be done for this man?" See David knew there was a reward. So, when they told him he could become the king's son-in-law- he thought that sounded pretty good, and he killed the giant (1 Samuel 17).

David was willing to fight for God's glory, but he wanted something out of it. God wants you to be willing to fight, and you should want something out of it too.

TOTAL VICTORY

What do you want from God? Do you want to see your son's and daughters saved? Do you want to see your family, friends, and everyone else filled with the Holy Spirit? GOD DOES.

God has a purpose for our being on the Earth; He has a mandate for His people. **God has called us to fight against evil and to be victorious in all our battles.**

To **pursue**, **overtake**, and **reclaim** is to carry out God's battle plan for his church. It is a **divine strategy for victory—IT CANNOT FAIL!**

The Invitation

Have you accepted Jesus into your heart? If not, today is your day to change your life forever by accepting the gift of salvation.

Pray this simple prayer:

Father,

I thank you for the gift of your Son, Jesus Christ. I ask Jesus to come into my heart now.

I confess with my mouth that Jesus is the Son of God. I believe in my heart that Jesus died for me on the cross, was buried, and was resurrected from the dead.

I repent of sin. I denounce the devil. Jesus take me as your own, live in me from this moment forward.

In Your Name,

Amen.

We believe that you have just taken a step that has changed your life forever.

We want to provide you with **Free Resources** to start you on your journey of faith.

Visit us online at bishopmerrittministries.org and let us know that you have accepted Jesus as your Lord to receive these resources today.

Dear Friend,

We are so grateful that God has given you an opportunity to read this book. We are confident that your life will be changed by the truths you have received.

If you desire to contact our ministry, you may do so by writing or visiting us online at:

> Bishop Andrew Merritt Ministries
> 10100 Grand River
> Detroit, MI 48204-0389
> www.bishopmerrittministries.org

If you desire to send a financial contribution, we will be most thankful for your support.

MAY GOD RICHLY BLESS YOU!

Bishop Andrew Merritt

www.ingramcontent.com/pod-product-compliance
Lightning Source LLC
Chambersburg PA
CBHW050608300426
44112CB00013B/2122